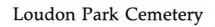

Loudon Park Cemetery

Entrance to Loudon Park Cemetery in the 1880s.

Loudon Park

Celebrating 125 Years

By– *Mary Ellen Thomsen*

BALTIMORE, MARYLAND

1979

PRESS OF SCHNEIDEREITH & SONS, BALTIMORE, MD.

CONTENTS

List of Illustrations

List of Illustrations *(Continued)*

Page

INTRODUCTION

For 125 years Loudon Park Cemetery has been a Baltimore landmark. Sheltered within its magnificent acres are more than 200,000 persons, many of whom played an important part in the history of the city, state and nation. Now the only extensive green area in the western part of the city, Loudon Park is one of the largest cemeteries in the world. The story of this historic institution—its past and its new developments to meet America's changing ideas of burial and memorialization—is the subject of this book.

Loudon Park Cemetery was founded in 1853, fifteen years after Green Mount Cemetery, the oldest in the city. Both responded to fill a new community need for a safe and beautiful place where loved ones could be memorialized and cared for in perpetuity. Churchyards, once the favorite choice, were running out of land. In addition many of them were in a dismal state of repair and lacking the necessary maintenance funds to do anything about it. The solution was for private companies to acquire and develop special tracts of land, selected for their location and beauty, and to manage them carefully as a service business.

Over the years Loudon Park became familiar to Baltimoreans. From its hills one could view the panorama of the city and harbor of Baltimore and the mouth of the Pa-

Just inside the Main Entrance in the 1860s.

tapsco River miles away. The woodland portions, with oak-crowned hills and dales, were as handsome as any public park, and picnickers flocked there. During the Civil War the government purchased a section for the Union Army and Southerners acquired a portion which became famous as Confederate Hill. Later the Federal government bought a portion on the eastern boundary which is now separately operated as the Loudon National Cemetery.

Loudon Park was always accessible. For many years Loudon Station was on the main line of the Pennsylvania Railroad between Baltimore and Washington. Caskets could also come on a special funeral car (remember *Dolores?*) which was in regular service with the city trolley system. Visitors could come by carriage or streetcar, and as the cemetery grew in size the management put in its own streetcar line, which operated from 1905 to 1931. The only such line ever running through a cemetery, it is still the subject of occasional feature articles, and has a special chapter in this book.

Almost every Baltimore family, humble or prominent, has a relative buried at Loudon Park, and it became the final resting place of many famous persons. Mary Pickersgill, who made the flag which flew over Fort McHenry in the War of 1812, is there. The son and two grandsons of Betsy Patterson Bonaparte and Napoleon's brother, Jerome, are buried there along with other family members. (Betsy herself is at Green Mount). There is the famous writer H. L. Mencken, often called "the sage of Baltimore," who achieved a national reputation as a critic of the American scene. And there is the World War II hero, Ensign C. Markland Kelly, Jr., for whom a memorial service is held by the American Legion every year.

In 1977–78, in an exhibit honoring the enterprising 19th century, the Maryland Historical Society featured firms at least a century old—firms which paved the way for the city we know today. The Society was not surprised to find that those firms which still survive are those that have been able to adapt to present times. It *was* surprised to find how many of the old Baltimore businesses are still controlled by members of the founding family.

The management of Loudon Park was not surprised in either case. It has been adapting to the needs of Baltimoreans for years. It had one of the first crematories in America. It had one of the first community mausoleums. It has a collection of outstanding memorials and private mausoleums. In 1971 it unveiled a master plan which included a magnificent chapel mausoleum and garden crypt complex to meet the needs of today—when the need for the traditional ten to twelve space family plot has almost disappeared and there is a national trend to pre-placed crypt entombment. With the opening of one of its most beautiful areas, Maiden Choice Run, in 1979, Loudon Park truly will become a full-service cemetery. In that section both crypts and a variety of memorial stones are to be pre-placed in the ground, a convenience for those in immediate need.

And as for founding families still in control? The Primrose family has played the major role in the development of Loudon Park Cemetery for 125 years. It expects to continue that way.

Chapter 1

How It All Began

THE LAND NOW OCCUPIED by Loudon Park Cemetery was originally part of the country home of one of Baltimore's most influential citizens, James Carey. Located on the southern side of the Frederick Turnpike several miles west of the city, it was a handsome, well-kept property. Many early accounts claim Carey named it Loudon Farms after Annie Loudon, a family slave. It is much more likely that it was named for a place of Carey's boyhood, and that Annie took her name from there also.

Backed by his wealthy family, James Carey made a fortune in the shipping business after the Revolution. His marriage in 1785 to Martha Ellicott, daughter of Nathaniel Ellicott, the owner of Ellicott's Mills, united two major Baltimore families. Among his other business activities, Carey organized the Bank of Maryland, later became its President, and served as a director of at least four other companies.

Active politically, he was elected to Baltimore's first City Council in 1797, and served intermittently until 1815. A liberal, he favored extending voting privileges, and is said to have devoted his last years to improving the lot of

Baltimore's Negroes. This, plus his wealth and business prominence, caused Carey Street in West Baltimore to be named for him. Carey died in 1834.

In 1853 one hundred acres of the beautiful estate Loudon Farms were sold to a group of prominent Baltimoreans. It was described as "part of a land situate on the south side of the Frederick Turnpike between two and three miles from Baltimore . . . sold by William E. Coale and other trustees to Gustavus A. Thompson by decree of the Circuit Court of Baltimore County in Equity January 12, 1853, and passed in a cause where William E. Coale and others were complainants and Isaac Coale and others defendants, and which was afterwards sold by the said Gustavus A. Thompson to James S. Primrose and others, the present proprietors."

The phrase "to James S. Primrose and others" is important, for it is indicative of the role the Primrose family played from the very beginning. The additional land acquired from time to time came mostly from adjoining estates of the Primroses—Beechwood, Pleasant Grove and Linden. Through 125 years, at least one Primrose family member, and usually several, have been associated with the company. It began with the first meeting of the Board of Managers, on February 22, 1853, "when James S. Primrose was called to the chair," and continues today when the president of the company is his great-great grandson, Harry C. Primrose, III.

Primrose Monument at Primrose Circle.

It is equally interesting, however, to note that seven of the eleven original incorporators can be identified as complainants or trustees in the 1853 case. There was one Carey, another James. There were four members of the Coale family (who were related to the Careys): James Carey Coale; William E. Coale; William Ellis Coale, Jr. and Isaac Coale, Jr. There was the Gustavus A. Thompson who sold the land to James S. Primrose. The other four men were John Q. Ginnodo, Elias Livezey, John McDowell, Jr. and George Ross Veazey. We know that Livezey, who came from Philadelphia to Baltimore in 1846, was a pioneer in Baltimore real estate, being one of the first to realize the coming importance of suburban real estate. He lived to be 102. Veazey was a lawyer, and the largest investor in the new enterprise, putting up $2,900. Messrs. Ginnodo, Livezey, McDowell, Primrose and Thompson invested $2,400 apiece; the others less.

The first Board of Managers consisted of six of these men, whose names were always listed with Mr. Primrose's first: James S. Primrose, Elias Livezey, John Q. Ginnodo, John McDowell, Jr., William E. Coale and Gustavus A. Thompson. At their first meeting they elected William Coale president and voted him a salary of $1,000 a year. Mr. Primrose was to be the secretary at $1,500 a year (the largest salary, probably indicating his colleagues' intention that his would be the major working office), and Elias Livezey treasurer at $1,200. All the salaries would have been considered good in 1853. The company expected to be a success.

The dedication, July 14, 1853, was all they could hope. Writing afterwards to the principal speaker, The Honourable Charles F. Mayer, a distinguished lawyer and former United States Senator, the managers expressed their

> . . . high appreciation of the Splendid Oration pronounced by you upon that occasion and their cordial and unfeigned thanks for the obliging manner in which you undertook the performance of a task which, to anyone less skillful and accomplished than yourself would indeed have been full of difficulties . . .

It had been a grand day, beginning with the Lord's Prayer and choir selections directed by a Mr. Mason, accompanied by the Independent Blues' Band. More than a thousand people attended, admiring both the oratory and the beautiful setting. Many of them were shortly to become lotholders in Loudon Park.

Chapter 2

The Early Years

AT THE END of its first year as a cemetery company, Loudon Park stated in its minutes:

> Resolved: that the affairs of the company are in a condition as favorable as can be expected in view of the mistakes made through inadvertence at the beginning of the enterprise, and that the consequences of these mistakes have been nearly overcome and are being obviated as rapidly as possible.

Actually it wasn't all that bad. A great deal had been accomplished. Plans were approved for a stone wall in front of the grounds, and a 2,000-foot ornamental railing. Picket fence was to surround the remaining sides and a gateway house erected for $2,500. An engineer was hired to lay out grounds into sections and lots, to grade the walls and walks, and to build bridges, culverts and dams. The Carey Schoolhouse lot, adjoining the cemetery, was to be bought if the price was not over $500.

Isaac Coriell was the first superintendent and general agent of the company to help the business committee, but within the year William May was elected superintendent at $1,100 a year. (Note that this was $400 less than Mr. Primrose was getting as secretary). Benjamin C. Barroll served a very brief time as the company's second president.

Lots were to sell at 25 cents a square foot until a thousand were sold. Lots were also given as dividends. This was to create a problem during the next few years when owners who received them that way resold at prices lower than the company's cash price. Fifty lots of 8 x 10 feet were donated to the Sunday School Union.

The second year office space was rented at 6 North Street. A special trip was made to Philadelphia to see the managers there "for the purpose of inducing them to take early measures to put up the gateway." The business committee reported that hands were to work from 7 a.m. until sunset with one hour allowed for dinner, and that in July they had agreed to work from 6:30 a.m. until 6:30 p.m. with an hour for dinner.

In 1855 General Henry A. Thompson was elected president. James S. Primrose resigned as secretary and was replaced by Stephen Pryor until Pryor was replaced by William F. Primrose (son of James) as secretary *and* treasurer in 1862. Also in 1855 the barn and stable were torn down, a new stable erected, and it was decided not to pay any commissions on the sale of lots. By 1857 the company had 277 lotholders, had dug 112 graves, and had an excess of $35.81 over expenses. Concerned about appearances, the secretary notified lot owners that they would have to remove wooden posts and rails enclosing lots, as regulations did not permit them.

Meanwhile Loudon Park was receiving removals from other cemeteries such as Baltimore Cemetery, Western, Universalist, Presbyterian Burial Grounds, Lutheran, Baptist, Whatcoat, Light Street, and St. Louis. Reporting twenty removals in 1858 for burial in Loudon Park, the minutes state immodestly:

> that six should have been from Green Mount Cemetery is a fact worthy of remark and a commentary stronger than any your Treasurer could make upon the high standing of your cemetery and the estimation in which it is held by the public.

Chapter 3

The Government Lot and Confederate Hill

THE DECADE OF THE CIVIL WAR began in the Loudon Park minutes with the report that the year just ended was "the healthiest known for long series of years; with an encreasing (*sic*) population the deaths have been 800 less than in previous years and of course decreasing the number of interments in the cemetery." How sad the directors would have been to foresee that the next general growth in population of Loudon Park Cemetery would come from the War Between the States. Eventually 2,300 Union soldiers and perhaps as many as 650 Confederate soldiers were buried there.

Maryland is often referred to as a "border state," and many people do not realize the enormous tensions this meant for its citizens. An enflamed group of them attacked the Sixth Regiment from Massachusetts in the city streets on April 19, 1861. The Mayor, George William Brown, and the Governor, Thomas H. Hicks, prevailed to help keep the state for the Union. President Lincoln was persuaded to move Union troops through Maryland avoiding the city. However, in order to insure the passing of troops and supplies, the Federal government took more and more control of the state and finally on May 14 occupied Baltimore.

Confederate Monument by Adalbert Volck.

Dissenters flocked to enlist in the Army of Northern Virginia. Many prominent men joined the 1st Maryland regiment, also called by its Revolutionary name, the Maryland Line. Although Maryland is usually listed as having provided 20,000 men for the Confederate forces, research indicates there were at least 22,000 in the Army and an unknown number in the Navy. Many enlisted in the units of other southern states, such as the First South Carolina Artillery, Regulars, in order to serve with friends or relatives.

At home, the families of these men found subtle ways to show loyalty to the Confederacy. Federal orders forbade the display or sale of badges of secession or such items as Confederate pictures, flags, music or even neckties. One ruling said that infants were not to wear socks in the red and white colors of the South. Deliberately provoking Federal authorities, some Baltimore belles took to wearing red and white rosettes in their hair and white aprons trimmed in red.

Official figures credit Maryland with 62,959 in the Union armed forces, of which 3,925 were in the Navy. Three important battles for the Union were fought in the state, and of course there were many raids and skirmishes. At South Mountain on September 14, 1862, General McClellan commanded the Union Army to check General Lee's attempt to invade the North. Three days later the bloodiest one-day battle of the war took place at Antietam, with

Confederate Hill after its restoration by the Daughters of the Confederacy.

many Maryland soldiers on each side among the 23,000 casualties. Taking advantage of Lee's retreat, President Lincoln issued the Emancipation Proclamation. The third major Maryland battle was at Monocacy Junction on July 9, 1864. Here the Confederates won, but their victory cost them a day's delay advancing on Washington, and heavy Union reinforcements arrived in time to save the capital.

On Christmas Eve 1861, about eight and one-half months after the beginning of the war, the *Baltimore Sun* reported on a cemetery for soldiers:

> A sanitary commission appointed to select a proper place adjacent to the city for the burial of deceased soldiers has reported upon the selection of a portion of Loudon Park Cemetery, and that selection has been adopted by those having authority in the matter. It is proposed for the purpose of erecting a monument on the plot, to permit the soldiers in the city and vicinity to subscribe ten cents, and the officers 25 cents each.

This lot became known as the government lot, and an army sergeant lived in a cottage nearby. By 1865 the government had a superintendent there, a William Heller, who in the eyes of the Loudon Park management was totally unfit: "He refuses to give information concerning the soldiers' graves . . . thereby preventing the making of a proper plot and designation of each grave and the name of the interred so that the authorities of the U.S. and all parties interested might be able at any time to find any individual interred and a proper Registration might be kept at each grave." However, Mr. Heller refused to give up either the papers or the premises and the company had to ask the government to remove him. In 1903 the government solved the problem by purchasing a 5.28 acre portion on the eastern boundary which included most of the Union burial plots. Other Union soldiers were moved there.

Now how did Confederate Hill get its name? Probably some Loudon Park lotholders sympathetic to the South offered their lots when the need arose. Eventually the cemetery traded lots with the deed holders and reburied them in one section. The first burials were in May 1862, one of a John Scott and one with the surname Graham, states and regiments unknown. Burials continued until August 1937 when Colonel Hobart Asquith, age 92, of the 1st Maryland Cavalry, became the last.

After the war, returning soldiers formed the Loudon Park Confederate Memorial Association. Since 1870 the southern exterior of the lot has been graced by the majestic marble figure of a Confederate soldier standing on a pedestal guarded by two angels with wreath and torch. The sculptor was Adalbert J. Volck. Many think the soldier is meant to resemble Robert E. Lee, but this was not intentional. Another monument was erected nearby in 1906 by the Ladies Confederate Memorial and Aid Society in Baltimore City, and dedicated to the memory of Confederate mothers and widows.

In 1871 another group of veterans formed the Society of the Army and Navy of the Confederate States in Maryland. Their first action was to try to return Maryland bodies from Virginia, and in three years they succeeded in moving 76. Additional ones were brought from other southern states.

In 1880 the Association of the Maryland Line was formed to care for the many Confederate soldiers who were now ill or destitute, often in almshouses. The state of Maryland gave them the Arsenal in Pikesville and $5,000 a year for the home. From 1888–1898 the home served 235 men. Of the 76 who died there, many were moved to the Confederate Lot. June 6 became Confederate Memorial Day, when the lot was the location for both a ceremony and a picnic. Old soldiers from the home, other veterans, and the band of the Dandy Fifth Regiment, resplendent in scarlet coats and towering helmets, took part. Services were conducted by Bishop William Dane, a veteran of the Richmond Howitzers.

This ceremony continued for years, but by 1932 there were only three Confederate veterans in the home, and it closed. Only the Maryland Division of the Daughters of the Confederacy continued to hold services there each year, placing a wreath of red and white carnations, and often serving iced tea, lemonade and cookies. The women became increasingly concerned about the poor appearance of the Confederate Lot. Graves had sunk and markers had fallen. Appeals to the War Department were turned down due to lack of funds. Starting in 1946, Mrs. Guy Hudson Parr led the Daughters in raising the necessary money, and Loudon Park did the work at cost. Each of the 605 known graves was leveled and reseeded and the stones were set in concrete.

Not all of the Confederate soldiers buried at Loudon Park are on Confederate Hill. Those buried elsewhere (many quite nearby) include Major General Charles W. Field, one of Robert E. Lee's best division commanders. In chapter eight we will hear more about Captain Frank A. Bond, Colonel Harry Gilmor, Colonel James R. Herbert, and General Bradley T. Johnson. Also, at the extreme southwestern corner of the Loudon National Cemetery, which joins Loudon Park on the east, is a rough-hewn stone monument erected by the U.S. government. It marks the burial place of 29 Confederate soldiers who died at Fort McHenry while prisoners of war, and of three camp followers.

Chapter 4

Till the Turn of the Century

MORE AND MORE the Primrose family dominates the growth of Loudon Park, although none served as president until 1901. William Fisher was president in 1864 and Charles Shipley in 1865, followed by General Henry A. Thompson again, who held the office this time until he died in 1880, for a total of 24 years. General Thompson was succeeded by George Gildersleeve, who served until his death in 1900. William F. Primrose was secretary and treasurer from 1867 until he died in 1891. He was succeeded by his son William D. Primrose, who had been assistant secretary. That same year another son, Harry C. Primrose, was elected a manager.

Although there was no perpetual care fund, the proprietors were careful to see that all lots were in good shape. The superintendent was charged to report yearly on the condition of lots "which may be so much out of repair as to detract from the general good appearance of the cemetery." Proprietors were to be notified and urgently requested to put these in repair. In case of gross neglect the Board of Managers could cause suitable repairs and charge the proprietor. This does not seem to have been a problem. Every proprietor had a ticket entitling him and his household to drive "with a carriage only" in the ceme-

The Cemetery's park-like appearance in the late 1860s.

tery, and many used this privilege regularly. One's lot, therefore, was on view all the time. In 1885 the cemetery announced that all lots sold from then on would be placed under perpetual care; a Perpetual Care Fund was added to the bylaws of 1886. Meanwhile the company would put neglected lots in order at $1.00 for a full lot and fifty cents for a half lot or fraction thereof.

Some typical prices from a booklet of 1880 were:

Digging adult grave	$4.00
Setting head and foot stones delivered on the lot	$1.50
Opening and use of public vault, one month	$4.50

The latter had been constructed in 1871 in a beautiful location with a stream and culvert. It is still in use today.

In 1885 the company began a series of land purchases. The first notice records land on the west and east sides from William F. Primrose "at a price paid by him with the interest 6% added to March 1st, 1885, and that the President be authorized to issue bonds for the amount. . . ." This was followed in 1890 by a much larger purchase: "from William F. Primrose all of his property known as Linden, lying west of the present cemetery property, including improvements, also the Hayes tract on Beechfield Avenue, the Harriet Calwell tract lying between Wilkens Avenue and the Old Maiden Choice Road and the Irving Bird lot corner of Frederick Turnpike and Loudon Avenue for $55,000."

More bonds were issued. It was then announced that in consideration of the purchase, William F. Primrose had agreed to lease the property for five years, paying $2,000 a year and having 1,795 voting shares. It was shortly after this that William F. died, and was replaced by his son, William D.

In 1889 Loudon Park formed a union with the Cremation Cemetery Company of Baltimore City, founded in 1885, selling it land for the erection of a chapel and crematory building. By the end of 1900, 176 cremations had been performed. This building served until 1974 when the new chapel mausoleum included a crematory and columbarium.

Visitors at Loudon Park near the turn of the century.

In 1895 Loudon Park made its last land purchase of the century, a small one. For $2,000 it was able to purchase two acres south of the cemetery bordering on Wilkens Avenue. This permitted extending Loudon Avenue to Wilkens Avenue for a direct entrance to the cemetery.

Rules remained strict. Visitors driving through the grounds were requested to walk their horses. Dogs were not admitted at all. Children had to be accompanied by parents or other proper persons, who were held responsible for their conduct. "No refreshments, or any party carrying refreshments, will be permitted to come within the grounds."

Rules for conveying building materials for lots and vaults were carefully spelled out. The management required that these:

> shall be introduced into these grounds, either on a broad wheeled cart or wagon, or by hand; to be first laid on the side of the road most convenient to the lot or lots to be enclosed, and from thence taken to the place required, either on wheelbarrow or by hand. Boards will be furnished to lay on the ground to prevent injury to the grass or walks; and the superintendent will give the necessary directions from time to time, as the case may require . . .

At first the company permitted individual taste in construction of monuments, reserving "the right to prevent the erection of large improvements, which might interfere with the general effect, or obstruct any principal view." But by 1895 with the new Mount Vernon section it stated that lots could only be improved by marble or granite posts and name stones and with limited flowers. Also there were to be no chairs or settees in this section.

As the cemetery developed more and more sections, a problem arose. How could the management be sure to be ready when a funeral party arrived at the gate? "Some undertakers are slow, some preachers talk longer than others, but sometimes you were surprised with an early arrival," remembers a long-time employee. The grave-digger might have finished and moved on—or he might still be working frantically.

The management solved the problem by ordering a 350-pound bell from the McShane Bell Foundry in Baltimore. Requested on October 3, 1898, it was "delivered by our wagon," according to the foundry, on October 15, and hung in a large tree. Each gravedigger was assigned a number, and the bell tolling that number of times alerted him when a funeral procession or florist wagon was arriving for the gravesite he was preparing. The bell was used until 1960, when the tree was struck by lightning. Restored in 1972, it hangs in a special mounting just inside

Bell formerly used to announce arrival of a funeral.

the Frederick Avenue entrance. Its peal can still be heard throughout the grounds.

As the twentieth century began, both Loudon Park and Baltimore were in excellent condition. The city census in 1900 was about 675,000. The cemetery had been founded "to provide for discriminating families a final resting place in a setting richly endowed by nature, where the memory of loved ones would linger forever." As its reputation spread, it was able to set prices which were within the means of many Baltimore families.

The Baltimore Federation of Labor History, published in 1900, had this to say about the city:

> No city in the world, the size of Baltimore, has a greater number of workingmen who own homes and no city can claim a more prosperous and thrifty class of working people . . . the cost-of-living here is low, less than New England, and fully 50% less than any other city . . . The city had a comparatively large growth in the past decade, larger than any other city in the South.

Touting industry in Baltimore, the booklet listed:

> . . . 1600 sailing vessels a year arriving and clearing for foreign ports
> . . . not a single banking failure in the last depression

... excellent railway facilities

... headquarters of the coal mining industry

... a city known for parks and beautiful residence streets

"The resident of the city," it concluded, "be he a working man with hands or brain, may have his own home, made attainable by the large industries, which are glad to exchange just coin for fair service and by low rents, and leave to own his own spot of ground he is then relieved from the system of tenant slavery to the common needs of life."

Many of these residents owned a second spot of ground at Loudon Park.

Chapter 5

Expansion Extraordinary

THE LAST DAY of the year 1900 brought the death of the president, George Gildersleeve, who had been with the company for 21 years, twenty as president. William D. Primrose, who had been secretary and treasurer, succeeded him as president and served as treasurer at the same time. The third of William F.'s sons, Frank, was now elected to the board and became secretary. This meant that there were three Primrose brothers among the six managers: William D., Harry C. and Frank.

Due to a series of deaths, the presidency was to change hands often over the next few years. William D. Primrose died in 1904 after serving three years and was succeeded by Henry F. Thompson, son of the former President, General Henry A. Thompson. Frank Primrose became secretary and treasurer, holding those offices until 1913, when he became treasurer only until 1918. In spite of poor health, he remained a director until his death in 1930. When Henry F. Thompson died in 1910, N.J. James was elected president; when he died in 1911, Francis Reeves of Philadelphia, a Primrose relative, succeeded him.

The first twenty years of the twentieth century saw the extraordinary expansion which put under one management the largest cemetery property in the United States. During these years Loudon Park acquired additional land, put in a private trolley system, formed the Overbrook Development Company, bought Druid Ridge Cemetery in Pikesville which was in the hands of receivers, and established a profitable greenhouse and nursery business which became Loudon Nurseries, Inc.

In 1902 the company sold its city office building at 323 N. Charles Street to T.W. Tongue Real Estate for $25,000. Immediately it bought for $35,000 some Primrose property known as Pleasant Grove, which was described as "lying on Wilkens and adjoining Linden." Two years later after the death of William D. Primrose it bought for $5,000 some small adjoining acreage from his estate to be used for single interments or small lots.

As early as 1904 the company was looking into the possibility of building a private railroad "or other means of conveyance to the new section," but decided to wait to clarify the intention of the United Railways and Electric Company in regard to extending the Wilkens Avenue Line. When it appeared that United Railways had no such plans, Loudon Park opened its own line November 14, 1905, with a luncheon for funeral directors at the Linden mansion, home of the Primroses. This venture of Loudon Park was so unusual and became so well known that the next chapter is devoted to it. That same year, 1905, the cemetery had recorded 20,000 lotholders and 50,000 burials.

A monument section around the turn of the ce

luding the large Wiessner Monument on the right.

Some members of the Primrose family were hired by the company for special jobs. For instance, in 1905 Harry C. Primrose was appointed consulting engineer at $500 a year but continued as a manager until his death in 1908. His son, H. Clay Primrose, was elected a director in 1916; that same year the company placed its greenhouse and nursery business under him at $1,000 a year salary and ten percent of all profits above $2,500. Two years later this business had grown so rapidly the company decided to separate it and incorporate it as Loudon Nurseries, Inc. H. Clay Primrose became its president, but also stayed as secretary of Loudon Park until he died in 1951.

Two major expansion moves were made in 1912. One was the formation of a corporation in the name of the Overbrook Development Company with an authorized capitalization of $50,000 for the purpose of dealing in real estate and the construction and erection of buildings. This new company was described as a suitable organization to purchase such lands of the Loudon Park Cemetery Company as were not necessary for its business.

The other expansion move, and one which received much more attention, was the purchase of Druid Ridge Cemetery in Pikesville. Founded in 1896 by a group of prominent Baltimoreans, Druid Ridge had been beset with financial problems. The managers of Loudon Park, who had been watching this develop for several years, tried to purchase Druid Ridge but were turned down. Shortly afterwards, however, stockholders of Loudon Park were notified that "interests closely connected with Loudon Park have purchased the Druid Ridge Cemetery and propose to turn it over to Loudon Park at cost." The notice described the property as located on the Reisterstown Turnpike a short distance beyond the city's northern limits in a large and rapidly growing community. The $220,000 price was considered low for the two hundred acres. Druid Ridge was described as doing a good business and serving an area which was not served by Loudon Park. The Board of Loudon Park became the Board of Druid Ridge and set about improving its new acquisition.

In more modest expansion, Loudon Park bought for $24,000 eighteen acres of the Herman Gerken property adjoining the Wilkens Avenue side of Loudon Park. About its only unsuccessful business venture was when its offer of $2,000 was not accepted for "the Crematory, Building and Good Will." Eventually Loudon Park did take over the crematory.

Several new managers joined Loudon Park who were to have long associations. William A. McLeran, who began with the company in 1902, was elected a manager in 1905. He served in many positions until his retirement in 1957 at the age of eighty, when he was elected vice president emeritus. Another long association, fifty years, was that of Morris A. Soper. Elected a director and vice president in 1913, he shortly became Chief Judge of the Supreme

Bench of Baltimore City. In 1917 he was elected president and served until 1950 and age 76. He continued as a director until his death in 1963.

With the purchase of Druid Ridge, the Board of Managers was expanded to nine directors: Francis Reeves, Francis Reeves, Jr., Dr. Joseph W. Hearn, Frank Primrose, German H. H. Emory, Robert D. Hopkins, Jesse A. Hitchcock, Morris A. Soper and William A. McLeran. In 1917 Mr. Reeves resigned, feeling that a local president was needed. As mentioned earlier, Judge Soper became president. Robert D. Hopkins was vice president, H. Clay Primrose secretary, and W. Smith Chambers, who was superintendent of Loudon Park, became treasurer. Arthur Koppelman joined the Board in 1918, replacing Mr. Hopkins as vice president when Mr. Hopkins died in 1921. Mr. Koppelman served as vice president until his death in 1953.

During the first part of the twentieth century, a number of cemetery associations were founded. Loudon Park was one of the early members of the Association of Maryland Cemeteries, founded in 1917. (One of its first rules was that of discontinuing the practice of holding funerals and making burials on Sundays). Over the years many members of the Loudon Park organization served cemetery associations. Most notable were William A. McLeran, who was founder and president of the Cemetery Association of Maryland and the District of Columbia for thirty years as well as president of the American Cemetery Association in 1945; and Robert T. Nuckolls, who in 1978 was president of the National Association of Cemeteries.

Chapter 6

The Loudon Park Trolley

RIDING THROUGH LOUDON PARK today, an observant visitor might catch a glimpse of steel rails or a roadbed hinting of some long-gone streetcar system. What could it be, he asks? Whoever heard of a trolley in a cemetery?

Loudon Park is the only cemetery in the world ever known to transport visitors through its grounds by means of its own railway system. And what an attraction it was, from the day of its opening November 14, 1905 (when the members of the Maryland Funeral Directors' Association were special guests for a trial run and a luncheon at the Primrose family mansion "Linden"), until it was replaced by a bus in the late summer of 1931.

Until the time of the Loudon Park trolley, the cemetery was well served by public transportation alone. On its eastern boundary was Loudon Station, one of the stops on the main line of the Pennsylvania Railroad between Baltimore and Washington. A casket could be delivered right to the cemetery, there to be met by a horse-drawn hearse.

More often, however, a casket arrived by special funeral car of the Baltimore city trolley system, run by the United Railways and Electric Company. The funeral director would make arrangements to have the *Dolores* (the Spanish word for sorrows) stop at the corner nearest the family home. The funeral party had to be ready on time so that the schedule could be maintained. Sometimes a band playing a funeral dirge walked ahead. The trolley ran on Frederick Avenue and over a short sidewalk to within a few feet of the cemetery. The casket was unloaded and pulled by hearse to the burial plot, while the mourners followed on foot. The *Dolores* went two blocks farther to a small car barn and waited for the return trip. On rare occasions another car, the *Chesapeake,* replaced *Dolores.*

But as the cemetery gradually expanded, the management began looking into the possibility of providing its own transportation within the grounds, both for visitors and for those arriving for a burial ceremony via the *Dolores,* who were still going to face a long walk within the grounds to reach the grave site. Providing its own line solved the problem. However, some used the vehicle for the sheer pleasure of a free streetcar ride, and there is an oft-told tale about a lady truant officer who used to cross the property in pursuit of her charges.

The one-mile line was erected by Messrs. Newhall and Company of Baltimore, and took three and one-half months to build. Starting at the main entrance of Frederick Road, it generally followed the streambeds, crossing a light steel bridge, toward the Wilkens Avenue side. Original plans had been to extend it to the new "Linden" property, and to provide service from the Frederick Road entrance to

The only cemetery in the world with its own trolley.

a new entrance on Wilkens Avenue. However, as the age of the automobile arrived, the need disappeared, and the extension was never built. Nor did the line ever connect to the United Railways system, which many thought would have been ideal, permitting the *Dolores* to come right into the cemetery. The *Dolores* was an unusually heavy car, and even though the United Railways and the Loudon Park lines had the same wide gauge, Loudon Park's light construction and bridge load limit meant the *Dolores* could not come inside the gates. So mourners arrived via the *Dolores*, and transferred to the Loudon Park line for the rest of the ride to the grave.

The Loudon Park line ran two single-track closed cars which had originally been horsecars. Later they were converted to trailers for cable cars on the Madison Avenue line of the Baltimore City Passenger Railway. Still later they were electrified and used until 1902 on the Orleans Street line.

The city system had given them only numbers—just like all their cars—and these were known as 2020 and 2021, but Loudon Park repainted them black with gold trim and lettered them as *Loudon* and *Linden* (the latter for the new section). Both had quartered-oak finish and velvet carpeting. The *Loudon* had large and comfortable wicker side chairs, but the *Linden* kept her lengthwise side-seating. Each car could seat thirty people.

An example of the magnificent commemorative statuary at Loudon Park.

For all but the last six months of its history, the cemetery line's chief motorman was Charles Caughey, grandson of the Baltimore businessman Noah Walker, who presented the city with the statue of George Washington in Druid Hill Park. Mr. Caughey had been working in the powerhouse of United Railways, which was where the Loudon Park line got its power.

Described as a diplomat, a fine gentleman, and a handsome figure at the controls, Mr. Caughey was a great asset to Loudon Park. He knew the location of many burial plots, and would often stop his car without being told. He carried a watering can for the convenience of passengers who wished to water flowers on the graves of loved ones. On occasional hot days he would come across boys hiking in some remote area, take pity, and offer them a ride.

In 1905 the *Linden* and the *Loudon* ran on a schedule, but soon a car was operated whenever there were passengers. Weekends and holidays were busy times, as many people arrived by carriage or streetcar bringing a picnic lunch and spending the day out with their families. But gradually the need for trolley service declined, and though a bus replaced it in 1931, a station wagon was sufficient a few years later.

John Horst, burial and memorialization superintendent and an employee of Loudon Park for 45 years, remembers vividly the decline in visitors. When the bus first replaced the trolley, perhaps 2,000 people a week were visiting, 1,500 of them on Saturdays and Sundays. "More came then in a week than in six months now. We had benches under the trees and the picnickers were very tidy." Four large greenhouses flourished, and sometimes the flower shop sold a hundred baskets a day. Mr. Horst drove the bus and later a station wagon as more and more visitors came in private cars. Today almost everybody comes by car, but if they don't the cemetery will still provide chauffeur service to their lots.

Chapter 7

Fifty Years of Progress 1920–1970

BY 1920 THE MANAGEMENT of the two cemetery companies was sufficiently complicated that a special operating committee was formed. From its minutes of that year we discover the following wages:

grave diggers	$25 per week
special laborers	$.45 per hour
lawn mowers	$.40 per hour
sicklers	$.36 per hour

We also come across the following intriguing report:

Mr. Llewyn suffered an accident in falling into a refuse container and wishes to know what to expect in regard to a settlement. Mr. Chambers was requested to ascertain what would satisfy him.

During the twenties new sections were opened with names like Holly, Maple, Myrtle and Juniper. The lake, which was polluted in wet seasons and almost empty in dry ones, was drained and replaced with a garden.

Flowers were always a feature at Loudon Park, largely due to H. Clay Primrose and a second Frank Primrose,

Another handsome piece of commemorative statuary.

nephew of Harry C. and son of his brother Frank. In 1931 the cemetery sold Loudon Nurseries to Frank Primrose, Jr., who operated it at Pikesville. The Board minutes carried a yearly resolution that he be authorized to operate it on the present basis . . . provided he shall report progress of the nursery business at the next regular meeting of the Board.

By 1937 the cemetery was considering developing nonmonument sections, which would provide a contrast to some of the crowded monument lots. These memorial sections, where graves are marked with bronze plates flush to the ground, are now found in the sections called Northlawn, Midlawn and Southlawn.

The thirties and forties showed such steady growth that by the fifties the operating committee was advising that additional ground would have to be developed to keep pace with lot sales. During these decades D. Luke Hopkins and Henry F. Walton became directors in 1931; S. George Wolf in 1938; Harry C. Primrose, III (great-great grandson of the founder), in 1946; Roszel C. Thomsen and Arthur Klinefelter in 1950. (Mr. Primrose and Mr. Klinefelter are the only ones still on the board today.)

Also in 1950 Judge Soper retired after 32 years as president. As mentioned previously, he remained another thirteen years as a director, making his total term an astonishing fifty years. His successor was Roszel C. Thomsen, a lawyer and former law clerk of Judge Soper's, who became a United States District Judge in 1954. Shortly after Judge Thomsen became president, Harry C. Primrose, III became secretary-treasurer. A year later G. Van Velsor Wolf replaced his father, S. George Wolf.

The supervisory jobs at Loudon Park remained in the same hands for many years, contributing to the successful operation. W. Smith Chambers was an employee, officer or superintendent from 1903 to 1947. After he retired Jesse Hitchcock served briefly as superintendent of both Loudon Park and Druid Ridge, but by 1952 Mr. Hitchcock was exclusively at Druid Ridge and George Craig Winterson took over as superintendent of Loudon Park, also serving as an officer, and staying until 1970. Mr. Hitchcock, who during 57 years served both companies as a director or treasurer, is primarily remembered as superintendent and later general manager of Druid Ridge.

As both cemeteries continued to expand, a new office building was constructed at Druid Ridge, and in 1957 the city office was closed. With this move came the retirement of Mrs. Elsie Duff, who had served Loudon Park and later both companies for a total of 39 years. (Her son, Barnard H. Duff, the director of services at Loudon Park, has been there for 23 years). Joseph Oliver became a director, and Francis B. Reeves retired after 45 years as a director.

In 1963 Judge Soper died, and Judge Thomsen had to resign as president because of a resolution passed at the Judicial Conference that no judge could serve as an officer, director or employee of a corporation organized for profit. Harry C. Primrose, III, who had been secretary-treasurer, became the new president. George E. Thomsen, son of Judge Thomsen and godson of Judge Soper, was elected a director and secretary. Fifteen years later Mr. Primrose and Mr. Thomsen still hold these offices. It is interesting to note that during these fifteen years only five new men served on the Board: Alfred M. Knapp, Jr., David de Villiers, Donald Primrose, William Primrose Sayler and H. Foster Walton, III. They are all related to the Primrose family. The tradition of family service appears likely to continue.

Chapter 8

Who's Who in Loudon Park

MOST BALTIMOREANS could easily identify at least two of the famous families whose last resting place is Loudon Park—the Pickersgills and the Bonapartes.

Mary Young Pickersgill is remembered by Baltimoreans for having made the "Victory Flag" which, flying over Fort McHenry in 1814, is said to have inspired Francis Scott Key to write *The Star-Spangled Banner*. A 30 x 42 foot fifteen-star flag was made of four hundred yards of hand-woven wool bunting. It was so large that it had to be assembled on the empty malt house floor of Claggett's Brewery. But at least some of it was made at the Pickersgill home on Pratt and Albemarle Streets, now known as the Star-Spangled Banner Flag House.

Mrs. Pickersgill, who was born February 12, 1776, and died October 4, 1857, was one of the early burials at Loudon Park. An old-fashioned slab of white marble was erected to mark her grave by her daughter Caroline, who was buried next to her mother in 1884. Flag-making was a tradition in the family. Caroline helped her mother with the Victory Flag. Her grandmother and Mary's mother, Rebecca Young, made the Grand Union flag of 1775 under which General George Washington took command of the American Army.

Mary Pickersgill, seamstress of "The Star-Spangled Banner."

Today 20,000 visitors a year visit the Flag House, making it one of Baltimore's foremost tourist attractions. For many years members of the Flag House Association have visited Loudon Park on Flag Day, June 14, to place a flag and memorial wreath on Mary Pickersgill's grave. The Association and The Society of The United States Daughters of 1812 restored the Pickersgill lot and rededicated it on October 10, 1978. In remembrance of Mary Pickersgill, the cemetery displayed a large fifteen stars and stripes flag on its own flagstaff.

The *Bonaparte* (sometimes spelled Bonaparti) family is known to Baltimore for romantic reasons: the love affair of Napoleon's brother Jerome with one of the city's fabulous beauties, Elizabeth (Betsy) Patterson. Though Betsy is buried at Green Mount Cemetery, her son and daughter-in-law and two grandsons plus five other family members are at Loudon Park.

Bishop John Carroll of Baltimore married Betsy to Jerome on Christmas Eve, 1803, when she was eighteen and he was nineteen. Napoleon was furious. The story in capsule has been stated as: "Jerome, bribed by his brother with a kingdom and a princess, basely deserted his American wife and became King of Westphalia." Nothing ever persuaded Pope Pius VII to annul the marriage and sanction Jerome's second marriage to Princess Catherine of Wurtemburg.

Monument to Napoleon's nephew, Jerome Bonaparte.

Jerome had already left her when Betsy bore their son in 1805, and named him Jerome Napoleon Bonaparte. The young Jerome never made much of a name for himself, although he was the first president of the Maryland Club in 1858. But he and his wife, Susan May Williams, had two sons who achieved prominence of their own. The eldest, also named Jerome Napoleon, graduated from West Point and had a colorful military career. Fighting in France in the regiment of the French Rifles, he distinguished himself in the Crimean campaign. His great popularity was a threat to the Bonaparte cousins, who were ruling France, and they would undoubtedly have been glad to get rid of him. However, the Prussians solved the problem for them when the Prussians overran France. Jerome, who had nearly starved during the siege of Paris, escaped to England. When he was able to get back to the United States he married Mrs. Edgar Newbold and settled down to a luxurious life on North Charles Street. City residents remembered them driving about in a carriage with the Bonaparte crest in silver, surmounted by the Imperial Eagle.

The second son, Charles Joseph, had a distinguished political career until his death in 1921. A leading Maryland Republican, he served as Secretary of the Navy and as Attorney General in the cabinet of President Theodore Roosevelt.

Every cemetery claims its war heroes, and Loudon Park

has them from each war fought during its 125-year history. As one might expect, many of the most famous fought in the Civil War and on the Southern side.

There was *Captain Frank A. Bond* (1838–1923), who fled Maryland in 1861 to serve the Confederacy under General Stonewall Jackson. In 1874 he became Adjutant General for Maryland, a post he held many times in addition to that of superintendent of the Maryland House of Correction.

There was *Colonel James R. Herbert* (1833–1884) of the 1st and 2nd Maryland Infantry, C.S.A. After the war he became the first commander of the 5th Regiment, Maryland National Guard, and served for seventeen years, from 1867–1884. He was also Police Commissioner for Baltimore City from 1877–1884, an interesting overlap of posts.

There was *General Bradley Tyler Johnson* (1829–1903), born in Frederick and a Princeton graduate of 1849. Johnson led the withdrawal of secessionists from the Democratic National Convention in 1860, after which he returned to Frederick and raised a company of volunteers at his own expense. He was one of the founders of the First Maryland Infantry.

Perhaps the best known of the Civil War heroes buried at Loudon Park is *Lt. Colonel Harry Gilmor* (1838–1883). His part in the war is so considerable that when he was captured for the second time in 1864, it was lauded by

Gilmor Monument with public receiving tomb in background.

Union General Philip H. Sheridan as marking the severing of the last link between Maryland and the Confederacy.

Harry Gilmor, of Glen Ellen on the banks of Loch Raven, was a handsome aristocrat who left home to enlist as a private in Virginia. He later organized and commanded the 2nd Maryland Cavalry, Army of Northern Virginia, C.S.A.

Gilmor was a skillful raider who reveled in commando-like tactics three-fourths of a century before they became popular in World War II. He led bands of rebels through northern Virginia, Maryland and Pennsylvania, destroying bridges, raiding supply depots, tearing up railroad tracks and cutting telegraph lines. In February 1864 he led one of his most famous raids on the B & O Line near Harper's Ferry, trying to prevent Federal reinforcements from arriving. On an isolated stretch of track he set up a log obstruction which brought the speeding train to a "crashing, crushing halt."

A handsome monument near Confederate Hill marks his grave. He is remembered also for his book, *Four Years in the Saddle* (1866), and for serving as Police Commissioner of Baltimore from 1874–1879.

There are many heroes from other wars. *Lt. John Ijams* (1789–1879) was one of the defenders of Baltimore in the War of 1812. *Lt. William Boone* (1871–1919) was in both the Lebanese-Turkish War of 1909 and World War I.

While on the battleship *Montana*, he participated in the rescue under fire of Armenians fleeing the Turks. In World War I he was boarding a captured U-Boat when it blew up and he was thrown into the icy waters of the North Atlantic. Picked up by a lifeboat, he continued his distinguished service through the rest of the war.

Lt. J. H. Mittendorff (1856–1923), who looked like Teddy Roosevelt and was nicknamed Teddy, was a hero of the Spanish-American War. While he was stationed on the battleship *Massachusetts* he risked court martial by attempting to stow away on the *Merrimac* and get involved in the real fighting. The *Merrimac* was sunk in order to block the mouth of the Harbor at Santiago, and Mittendorff escaped with a reprimand.

Ensign C. Markland Kelly, Jr. (1916–1942) was piloting a single-seater plane when he was shot down in the battle of Midway, June 4, 1942, in World War II. His body was never recovered. His grieving father, owner of the automobile agency Kelly Buick, Inc., and a former president of the City Council, vowed the son would not be forgotten. He founded the Ensign C. Markland Kelly, Jr. Memorial Foundation. In 1952 the American Legion erected a marker on young Kelly's grave, and the following year began holding services on Memorial Day.

Another sea hero, though not at war, was *Captain F. W. Hamilton Murrell* (1862–1916), who is credited with a

— A MEMORIAL —

ENSIGN C. MARKLAND KELLY Jr. USN
BORN SEPT. 22 1916   DIED JUNE 4 1942

IN MEMORY OF AN AMERICAN YOUTH WHO GAVE
HIS LIFE TO HELP PERPETUATE THE IDEALS THAT
MAKE AMERICA GREAT

GREATER LOVE HATH NO MAN THAN TO
LAY DOWN HIS LIFE FOR HIS COUNTRY

LOST IN ACTION IN A SINGLE SEATED FIGHTER
PLANE IN THE BATTLE OF MIDWAY JUNE 4 1942.
HIS BODY WAS NEVER RECOVERED FROM THE PACIFIC

Memorial to World War II hero, Ensign C. Markland Kelly, Jr.

dramatic sea rescue when he was only 27 years old. Murrell was commanding the steamer *Missouri* of the Atlantic Transport Line. On his way from London to Philadelphia and Baltimore, he sighted the steamer *Denmark* from Copenhagen in distress. Murrell, whose boat had room for only twenty passengers, threw his entire cargo in the sea and took on all 733 crew and passengers of the *Denmark*. On his monument at Loudon Park is the inscription, "And Every Soul Was Saved."

Of the many others buried at Loudon Park who contributed to the quality of life we can mention only a sampling. Here are some drawn from the fields of arts and letters:

Charles Weber (1855–1947) is remembered as developing the Old Fifth Regiment Band from a small unit into an organization of 145 pieces that gained nationwide recognition. His mausoleum is mentioned in the next chapter;

Frederick R. Huber (1884–1959), managing director of the Lyric Theater from 1921–1959. He had a singular effect on Baltimore music from 1916–1942. Through his efforts the Baltimore Symphony was organized as the nation's first symphony supported directly by city tax funds. He became municipal director of music, the first position of that kind in the nation;

Ottmar Mergenthaler (1854–1899), for whom the vocational high school is named. A native of Germany who

Charles Weber Mausoleum.

was trained as a watch repairman, he came to Baltimore in 1876 and here perfected a machine for making slugs, each one of which could do the work of a line of type set by hand. His Linotype, which was patented in 1885, created a revolution in printing. Unfortunately, Baltimore newspapers were afraid that installing the new machine would cause typesetters to lose their jobs, and so New York gets credit for installing the first one.

Frank R. Kent (1877–1958), a reporter and editor who helped found the *Evening Sun*. He is remembered as author of *The Great Game of Politics*, which was also the name he used for his newspaper column.

And last of all but perhaps best known is *Henry Louis Mencken* (1880–1956), internationally recognized as a critic of the American scene. His biting wit and genius for ridicule did not always make him popular. He started his career on the old *Morning Herald* as a reporter, later becoming editor of the *Evening Herald* before moving on to the *Sun* and the *Evening Sun*. It has been said that his treatise *The American Language* assures him a place among philologists. The Enoch Pratt Library holds open house in the Mencken Room each year to mark the anniversary of his birth, September 12. Members of the public come from near and far for that one day.

Ottmar Mergenthaler, inventor of the Linotype machine.

Chapter 9

A Groundsman's Delight

MAINTAINING THE GROUNDS at Loudon Park is a tremendous task. It takes 32 employees in summer and seventeen in winter, not counting the fourteen members of the burial crews. Since 1977 this effort has been directed by Robert C. Larsen, operations manager, a licensed arborist with degrees in agronomy and ornamental horticulture from the University of Maryland.

"I came from Johns Hopkins because this job is such a challenge," says Mr. Larsen. "My first priority is to improve the looks of the cemetery, section by section, to make it even more attractive." His second priority is to eliminate weeds. Next, worn-out obstacles to mowing, such as old marking posts belonging to the cemetery, must be removed and replaced with flush markers. Last, a tree program will remove yearly about two hundred of the short-lived or weak-rooted trees and plant more durable ones.

The work is harder because over the years in a cemetery of this age monuments collapse, graves sink, and about a quarter of the area is not accessible to modern equipment. Even today, one in twenty graves must be dug by hand. But one of the rewards for painstaking work is coming

AUGUST MENCKEN
JUNE 16 1854 —— JANUARY 13 1899
ANNA MARGARET ABHAU MENCKEN
JUNE 11 1858 —— DECEMBER 13 1925
SARA POWELL HAARDT MENCKEN
MARCH 1 1898 —— MAY 31 1935
MARY EYER KLINE MENCKEN
JANUARY 24 1888 —— OCTOBER 13 1940
HENRY LOUIS MENCKEN
SEPTEMBER 12 1880 —— JANUARY 29 1956
ANNA GERTRUDE MENCKEN
NOVEMBER 17 1886
AUGUST MENCKEN
FEBRUARY 18 1889 —— MAY 19 1967

Mencken family ledger tomb.

Groundskeeper of 1860s with Patapsco River in background.

across the many beautiful, unusual and historic monuments in the cemetery; no one knows more about them than the groundsmen. They are the ones who once found a candle stub and canned food indicating that someone had broken into a mausoleum and set up housekeeping. They are the only observers of an occasional gypsy funeral, where before the coffin is closed, extra clothing, money, and wine are thrown in. They are the ones who discover and deplore that once again vandals have painted red the toes and fingernails of a graceful statue of a woman sitting upon a family monument. They set things aright because they really care, and tomorrow may bring again the joy and surprise of something heretofore undiscovered.

The very oldest part of the cemetery is a small, family graveyard where James Carey, the original proprietor of Loudon Farms, is buried next to his wife, Martha, and four other relatives. However, in sections such as Whatcoat there are even older stones—originals which were moved years ago when some entire church cemeteries were removed to Loudon Park. Some are still family plots of as many as a dozen or more graves enclosed by iron fences. Others have sunk and grass has grown around the edges, but careful cleaning and clipping have revealed memorials like this one:

STRIND

Born October 1795

Drowned by the upsetting of a boat between Fells Point
and Ft. McHenry

or (1801)

She was a loving wife and a tender and a good neighbour

The theme of beloved spouse or parent carries on throughout the years. The most unusual example is two huge limestone slabs or ledger tombs set with headstones to resemble beds for the graves of James Wesley Mc-Gready and his wife, Elizabeth Martin. She died in 1889; he in 1900. Her inscription reads, "At rest in her little home."

Portion of Carey family ledger tomb.

Another man is buried between two wives. The stone for the first, who may have died in childbirth, reads, "A Martyr to Motherhood," while that for the second says, "Faithful Unto Death."

Here is one which honors both parents:

Father
Life of Seeds, Roots
and Caring

Mother
She Still Remains in
Our Hearts

Two more recent ones read:

To Pop on Father's Day
Earl W. _____

1902   1973

and

William A. _____
December 25, 1964
Christmas When All My Lights Went Out

It is not as unusual as one might think for a lot owner to erect a stone with the inscription completed except for the date of death. Two of the groundsmen's favorites read like this:

William O. — [he died 1977]
Father — Lover
and My Man

Mildred — [still living]
Mother, Companion
and All Woman

and

Floyd L.   1919 –   Elsie D.   1921 –
Out on Friday Night

Many stones in Loudon Park bear the emblems of fraternal organizations, such as the Shriners or Knights of Columbus, or of trades and professions. There are anvils, chains, anchors, military insignia, and balance scales. Perhaps the most unusual is a monument topped with a fireman's helmet and inscribed:

To the memory of my beloved husband
John Acomb
Who lost his life in the
Sharp Street Fire
September 2, 1888
Aged 35 years

Other monuments bear mute witness to those who died in battle. There is Samuel T. Walcott (1830–1884), killed

Acomb Monument with fireman's helmet.

at the battle of Custer's Little Big Horn. There is Pfc. Donald Rothe, USMC, 1925–1945, killed at Iwo Jima, whose stone has in relief the scene of the flag raising so often shown in historical accounts and is inscribed:

He held his ground with steadfast soul

A ceremony is held every year at his grave.

An impressive looking stone to Joseph R. Stonebraker reads:

The bearer, Joseph R. Stonebraker, Co.C. 1st Md. Cavalry,
having done his duty faithfully to the present time,
is permitted to go where he pleases until called for.

C. W. Dorsey
Lt. Col. Commander,
1st Maryland Cavalry, C.S.A.

But how did Moritz Zetsch die, the groundsman wonders? His stone reads:

Born February 18, 1857
Murdered January 1, 1887

Probably not in a war—the date doesn't fit. Was he killed in cold blood or defending himself?

Perhaps the most beautiful monument in the cemetery, and one of the largest, is that of the Wiessner family of

The William Wilkens, Jr. Mausoleum at Mount Vernon Circle.

the brewery company. The marble for it came by boat from Italy, and there is a significant amount of hand-carving of the figures on it. Located on a slight knoll, it has long been an attraction for visitors, many of whom sit on its steps.

The cemetery also boasts a large number of handsome private mausoleums. Two particularly handsome ones are memorials to the Kriel family (meatpackers) and to Charles Weber. The Weber mausoleum is approached through a double row of Japanese hollies. The structure for this famous bandleader includes his likeness in stained glass.

The William Wilkens mausoleum belongs to the German family which came to this country in the 1840s and established a hair factory on Frederick Avenue. Wilkens Avenue is named for them. A second and more beautiful Wilkens mausoleum, located at Mount Vernon Circle, is a memorial to William Wilkens, Jr. and his wife's family. It is made of an unusual type of granite no longer available.

But perhaps the most striking mausoleums are those of the Fitzgerald and the Weiskittel families. The Fitzgerald mausoleum lot (Richard B. Fitzgerald, 1807–1867, was a sea captain and an owner of the Booth-Fitzgerald Company) is beautifully landscaped and decorated with handsome statues of Jesus and the Angel Gabriel, and also with enormous Grecian-style urns on pedestals. One of the oldest mausoleums, it was pictured in all of Loudon Park's

Fitzgerald Mausoleum, one of the most striking in the Cemetery.

early promotional material. Each winter the statues are encased in plywood boxes.

The Weiskittel mausoleum is made entirely of cast iron, painted in silver. It was a fitting material for the family, which had been in the stove manufacturing business since 1850 and before that in Germany. This structure is so unusual that it has been accepted for the National Register of Historic Places.

Two monuments at Loudon Park with especially poignant tales behind them are the memorial to the Evening Sun News Boys' Band, and the William H. Larrimore memorial to his sweetheart.

The Sun Boys' Memorial is to five members of the band who lost their lives July 4, 1924, when the steamer *Three Rivers* caught fire on the Bay of Baltimore. The band was returning from playing for the workboat races in Crisfield, and everybody was in bed when fire broke out shortly before midnight. The boys, under the leadership of their director Frank "Pop" Morse, were very brave. The older boys helped the little ones, and also aided women and children to escape. But five boys between the ages of thirteen and seventeen were never seen alive again. Their memorial reads:

> They have all moved a little closer to the
> Master of all Music

Silver painted, cast iron Weiskittel Mausoleum.

Sun Boys' Memorial.

The Larrimore monument, in the Cedar section, is the subject of a romantic tale with an uncertain ending. It is a six-foot shaft topped by a two-foot angel, its right arm (now broken) pointing to the adjoining lot. In the midst of the inscription is the outline of a hand also pointing to the adjoining lot. The inscription reads:

Lillian
Estella Barton
Born
June 4, 1892
Died March 1, 1922
This tomb is erected
here for Estella who
is in the next lot
It was objected to
being put on her grave

Presented to Estella
by
William H. Larrimore, her friend

The cemetery records that Estella died of sleeping sickness at age 29. A grieving Larrimore wanted to erect a monument on her grave, but her parents refused to allow it. Finally her father and uncle signed a court order restraining him. Her parents put *nothing* to mark the grave, so Larrimore purchased the adjoining two-plot lot and erected his monument with the right arm extended toward

Monument to Estella Barton, "who is in the next lot."

Estella's grave. He never used his lot. Estella's parents and her brother were later buried with her in the Barton lot, but there are no markers for them, either. It is just a four-grave plot of grass.

What happened? Lou Azrael in the *News-Post* of 1938 interviewed Larrimore, who was married and had three children and didn't want to talk about Estella. The *Sunday Sun* of January 12, 1974, ends its account like this:

> Nobody has ever been seen visiting either lot.
> Did young Larrimore find another sweetheart and
>   live out a happy life?
> Or did he die, alone, unidentified, and heart-
>   broken in some faraway corner of the world?
> Who shall say?

These are just a few of the many interesting markers a visitor might want to locate. The cemetery employees are happy to help. They are proud that Loudon Park was chosen to be featured in the Bicentennial television spots of famous Baltimore landmarks. They will show you the section where they prepared a special "grave" for filming a burial scene of Walt Whitman's mother in the film about the famous American poet. Loudon Park was chosen for its beautiful setting and the style and dating of the monuments. The film crew was impressed with the tranquillity of the spot, and delighted to catch snatches of birds trilling. The groundsmen appreciate these every day.

Chapter 10

A New Look for Loudon

KNOWING THAT NO SUCCESSFUL BUSINESS can afford to stand still, the Loudon Park Cemetery Company began to look to the future. Its financial position was strong. Its location, now the only large green area west of the inner-city, was in its favor. Green Mount, always its major rival, had run out of space. Loudon Park still had plenty of space. What was the best way to use it?

It was apparent that Americans' ideas of burial were changing. Family members were scattered all over the country now. Whereas heads of households had formerly purchased lots with spaces for perhaps a dozen graves, today they were more likely to want two, or four at the most. It was not practical to own a large plot of ground. Additionally there was an emerging trend toward above-ground entombment. Long the choice of royalty and other famous persons, it could now be brought within the financial means of many people. With modern methods, it could amount to no more than the complete costs for traditional ground burial.

In 1968 the management consultant firm of Coffay, Marshall Associates Inc. of Baltimore was hired to assist with long-range planning. Clyde T. Marshall, certified management consultant, shortly became the senior executive vice president for both Druid Ridge and Loudon Park. Robert T. Nuckolls, a nationally recognized leader in the marketing of cemetery property and services, was brought in 1972 from Nashville, Tennessee, to become vice president of marketing and later executive vice president and director of marketing.

In 1971 the company announced an extensive modernization program. Its first phase was to be a chapel mausoleum and garden area designed by Harley Ellington Associates of Detroit, Michigan.

A chapel mausoleum and garden complex provides both above-ground and below ground pre-placed crypts. Those above ground, often referred to as community mausoleums (to distinguish them from those built by private families) may be in closed buildings or in covered areas. The body, in a casket, is placed in a wall crypt; the opening is sealed and covered with a crypt front with bronze lettering. There are columbarium niches for cremated remains and chapel areas for committal services.

The garden area of a mausoleum complex features pre-placed underground lawn crypts over a drainage system. There are no monumental stones, only bronze markers flush to the ground, so that the entire expanse is an attractive and peaceful memorial garden, with extensive landscaping.

Main building of new Chapel Mausoleum complex.

Loudon Park's new chapel mausoleum was built facing the cemetery's Wilkens Avenue gate. Constructed of granite and Maryland stone, it was designed by Malcolm B. Stirton, A.I.A., president of Harley Ellington Associates. The main building holds six levels of crypts attached to a modern chapel structure. Its overhang acts as a partial shield against the elements. Over the entrance to four different chapels are limestone carvings signifying their names: Chapel of the Roses, Chapel of the Pines, Chapel of Peace, Chapel of Memories. Floor to ceiling windows are of an unusual faceted glass and were designed by Conrad Pickel Studios of New Berlin, Wisconsin.

Wrote Ruth Heird, editor of the cemetery newsletter *The Epitaph:*

> Easily visible from Wilkens Avenue, the structure makes an impressive silhouette against the sky as it sits perched on the crest of a hill with a backdrop of large, stately trees. As you walk beside the huge granite crypt walls and tall columns, a feeling of majestic solemnness and serenity engulfs you. The chapel motifs are represented in floor to ceiling windows of colorful faceted glass. Glimmering as the sun streams through, the windows are truly works of art and make beautiful settings for services of any denomination. The crypts are marked with bronze lettering, mak-

ing the inscriptions neat and dignified. This mausoleum offers above-ground entombment with the feeling and beauty of nature present at the same time, a combination I find most attractive . . .

The new garden area, covering an acre, has the natural beauty of an outdoor garden. Unseen beneath the ground are 1,800 double depth pre-placed modular units of reinforced concrete which will stay clean and dry. Those who prefer traditional ground burial can now have it in a very modern manner. In the center of the garden is a beautiful sculpture, The Crown of Eternal Life, by the internationally known artist, Jean Ferre Barberi.

Finally, in 1974, in keeping with its policy of offering the public as many choices as possible, Loudon Park opened a new division, headed by James R. Thomas as Director of Memorialization. Upright monuments of granite or flush memorials of granite and bronze could be purchased right at the cemetery, relieving the bereaved of another burden during an already difficult time.

Thus now with the opening of its chapel mausoleum complex, Loudon Park truly became a full-service cemetery, offering any form of burial or entombment. Those who prefer traditional ground burial with traditional monuments could now even buy those services all at one time, since the new Maiden Choice Run section afforded pre-placed crypts and pre-placed monuments in a variety of styles. The cemetery had had a crematorium on the premises since 1889; now these services were located in the building with the chapels. Once considered a stately monumental cemetery where imported marble sculpture was the ultimate status symbol, Loudon Park could now also be considered the most up-to-date cemetery in Baltimore.

Conclusion

"I have many early memories of Loudon Park," muses today's president, Harry C. Primrose, III, great-great grandson of the founder. "I can remember at age four visiting 'Linden,' my great-grandfather's place—a big Victorian house with a widow's walk but no electricity or heat." Three large Primrose homes remained inside the Wilkens Avenue gate for many years even after much of the family property was sold or leased to the cemetery.

"My father, H. Clay Primrose, was always involved with the company. I remember when he'd bring home a $10 gold piece—no bigger than a dime—from a board meeting." Although his father was a civil engineer and landscape architect engaged in many projects other than Loudon Park, young Harry always sensed that the cemetery was a major interest for the family and many relatives. He was pleased to be elected a director in 1946, secretary in 1952, and president in 1963.

"When I was a boy I considered it a great treat to talk to the engineers when they stopped for lunch at the spur of the Pennsylvania Railroad on the cemetery grounds. I guess you could say even then I knew the business was important to our families' livelihood, but that we were also providing an important service to the community we all knew and loved. I hope we can keep it that way . . . for another 125 years . . . and more."